# TRAIN
## COLORING BOOK

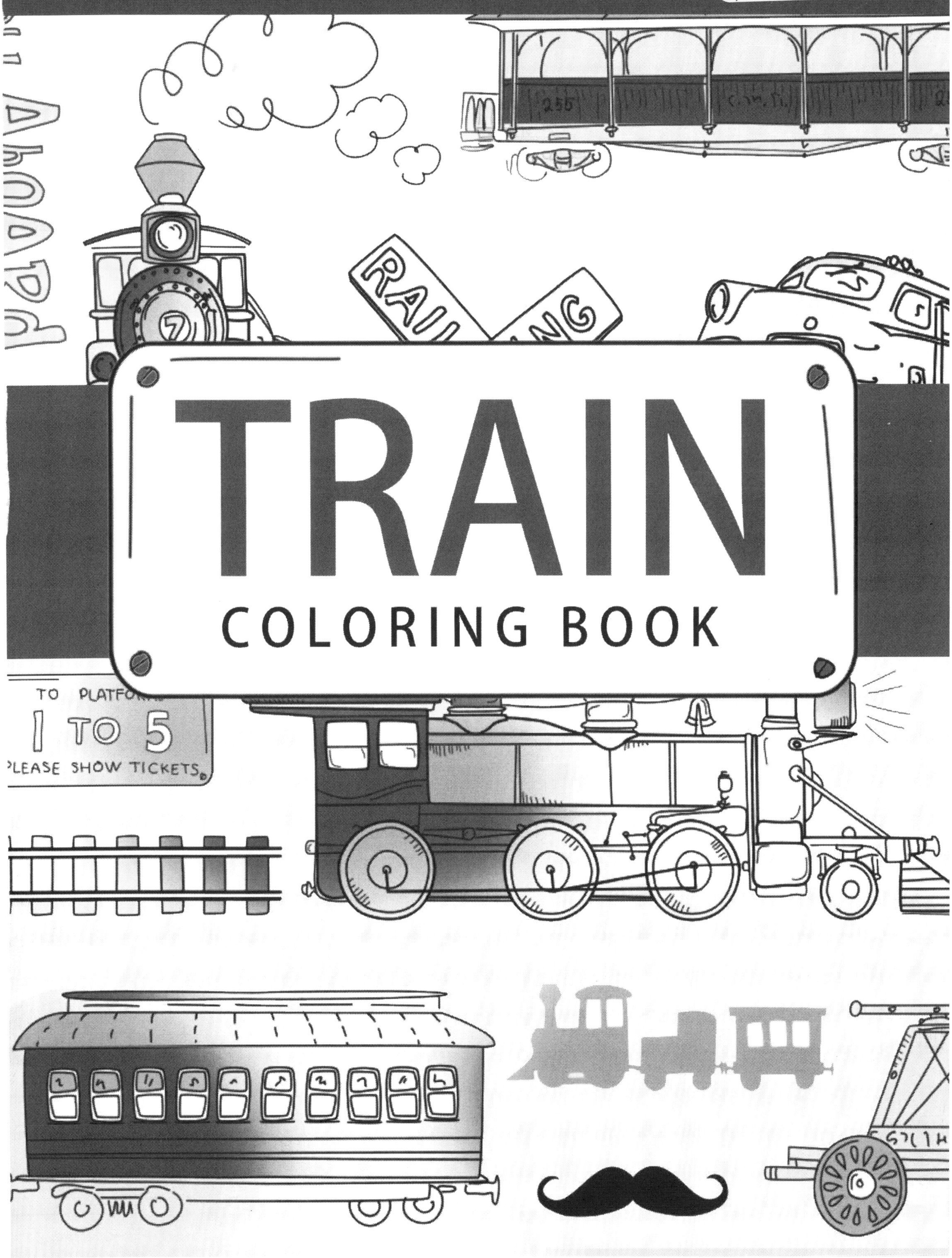

# COLOR TEST PAGE

# COLOR TEST PAGE

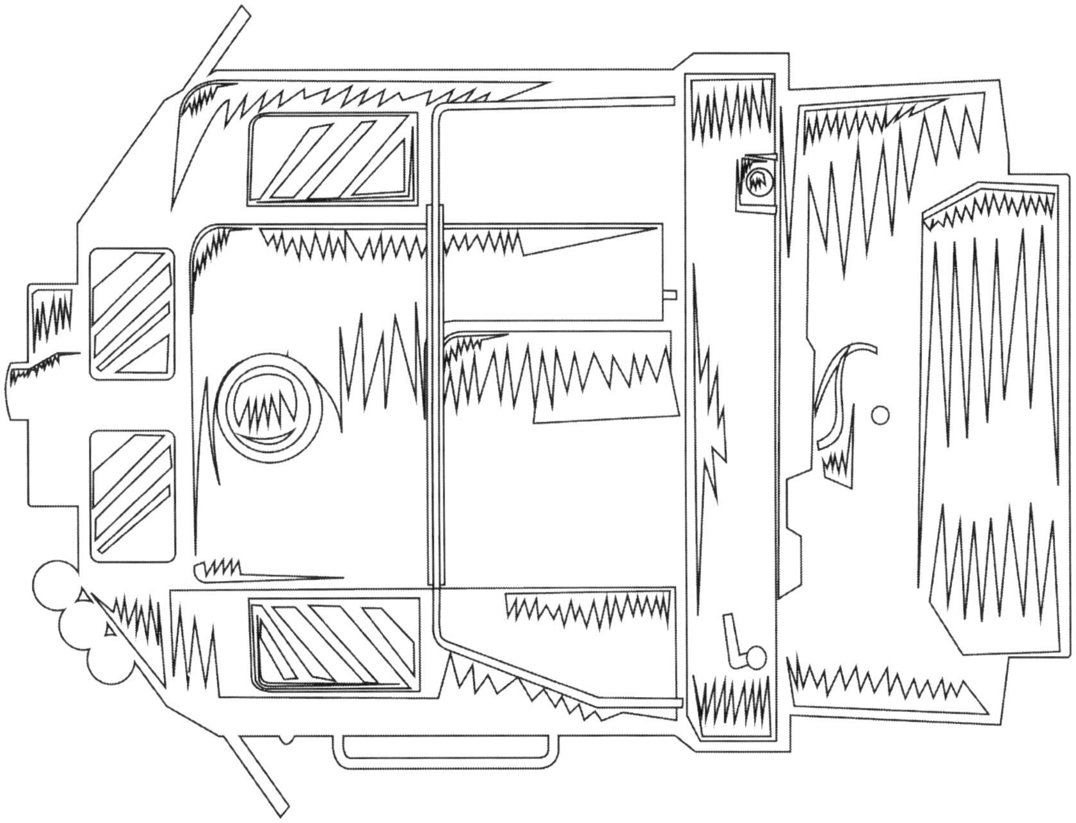

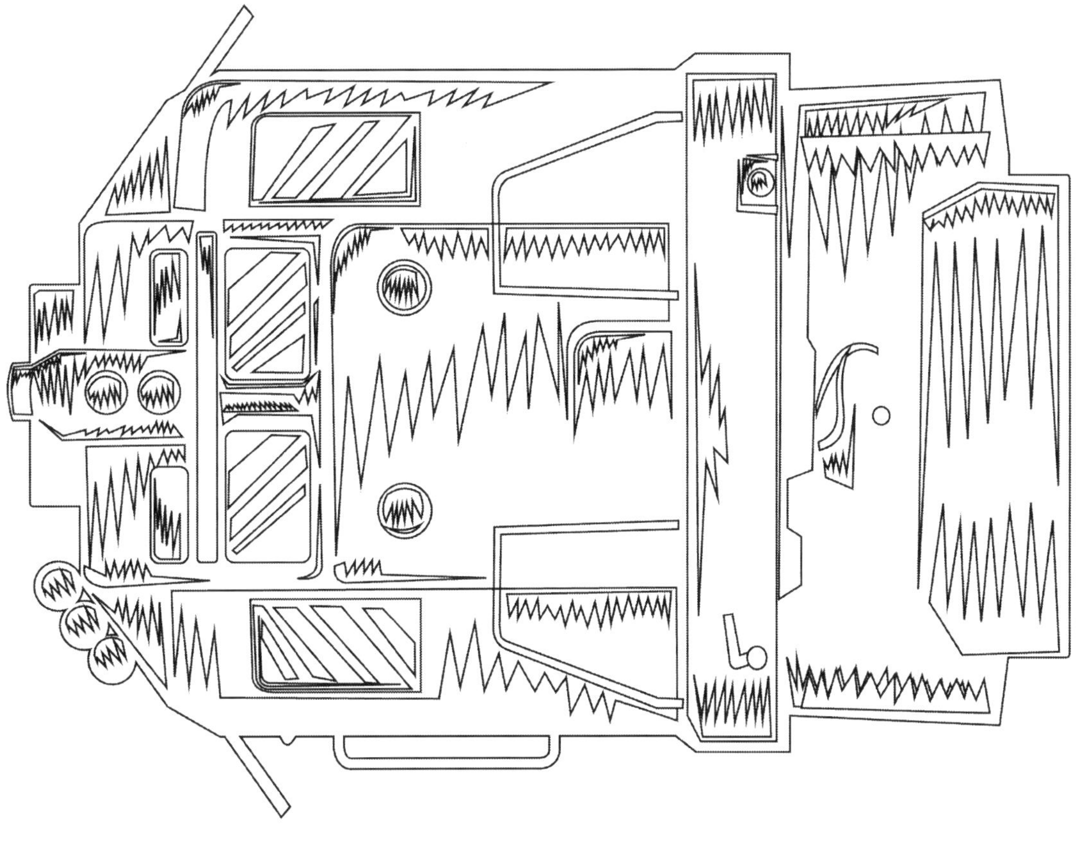

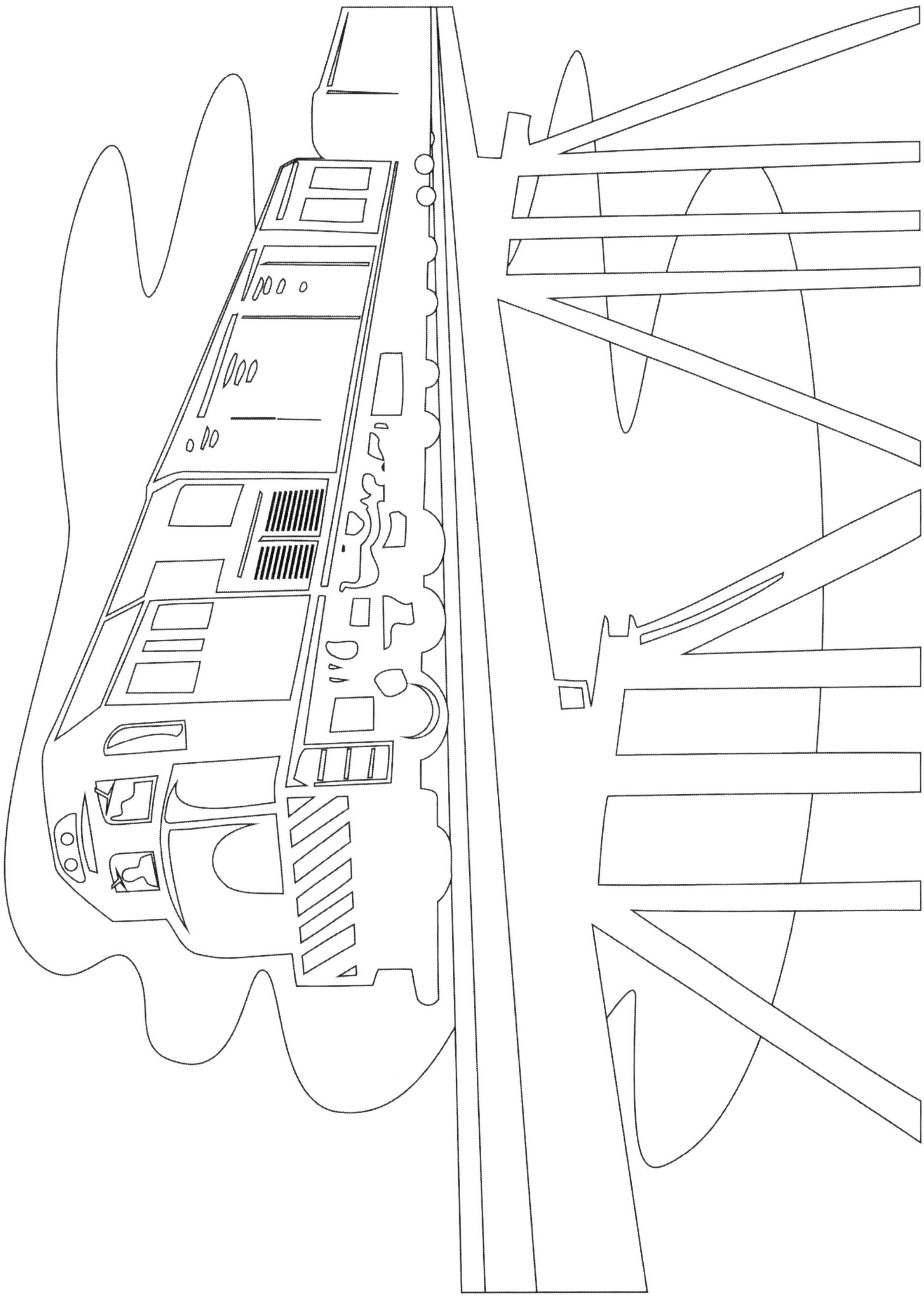

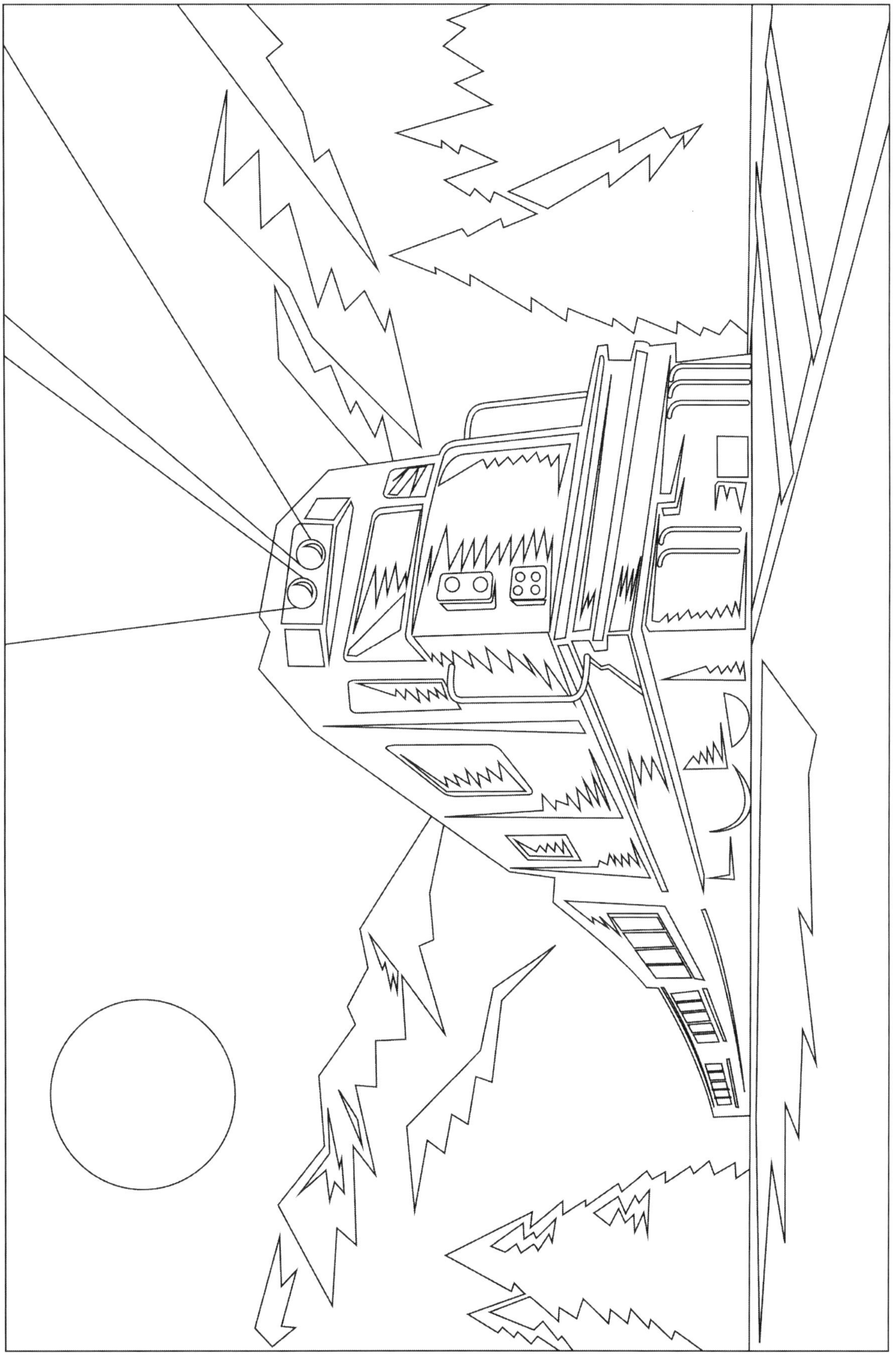

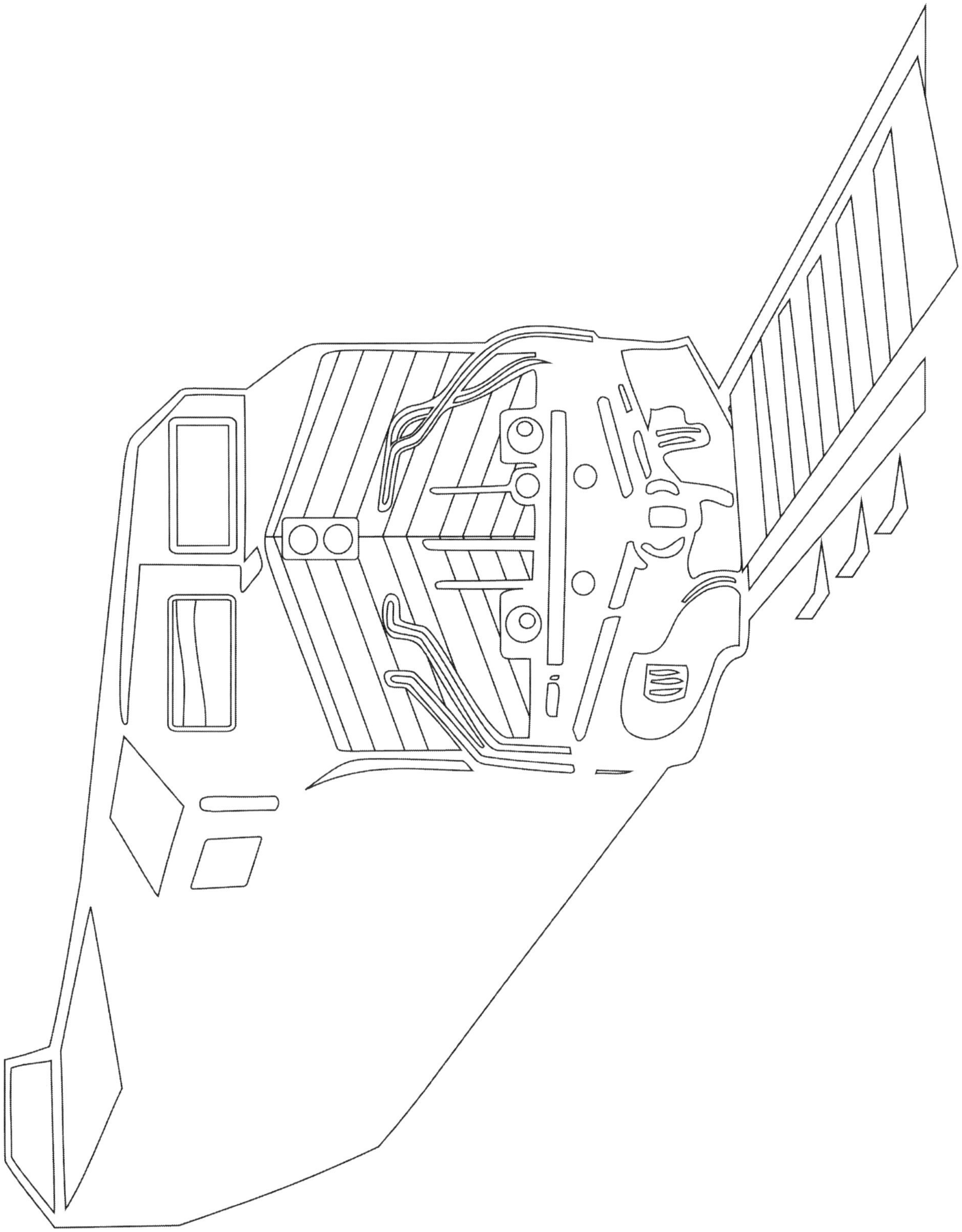

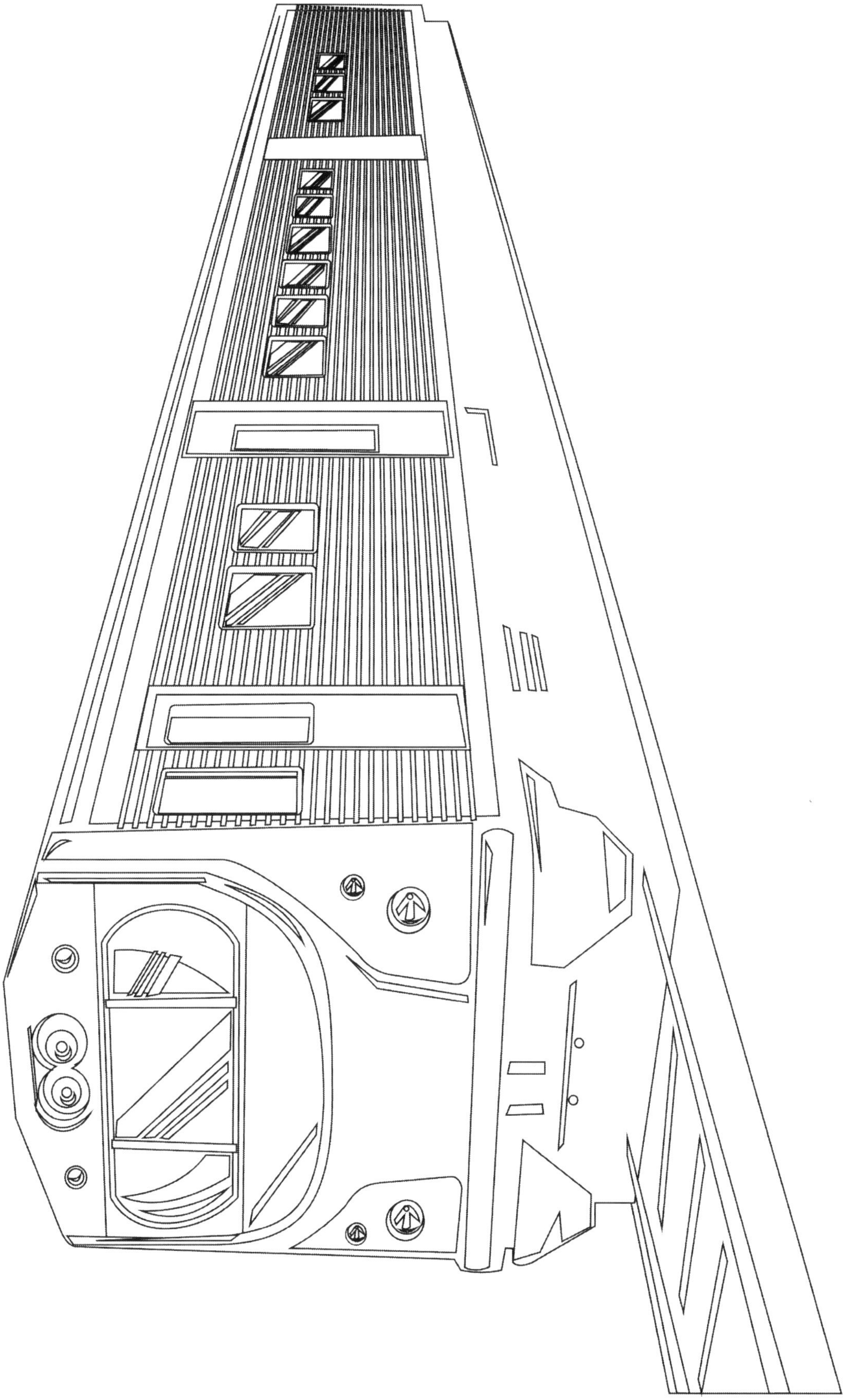

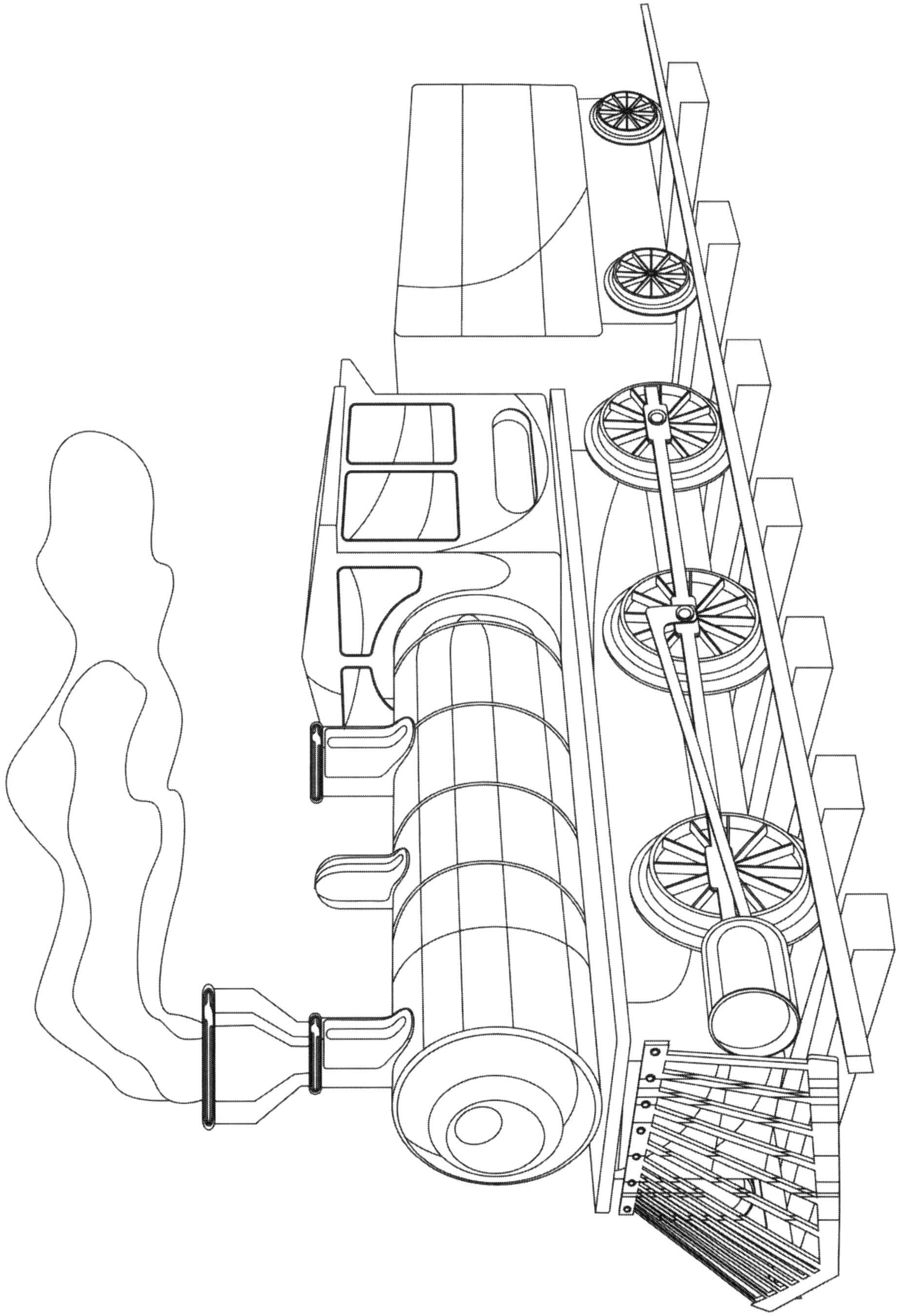

all Aboard
CENTRAL STATION
RAIL ROAD
CROSSING
CHOO! CHOO!
TO PLATFORMS
1 TO 5
PLEASE SHOW TICKETS

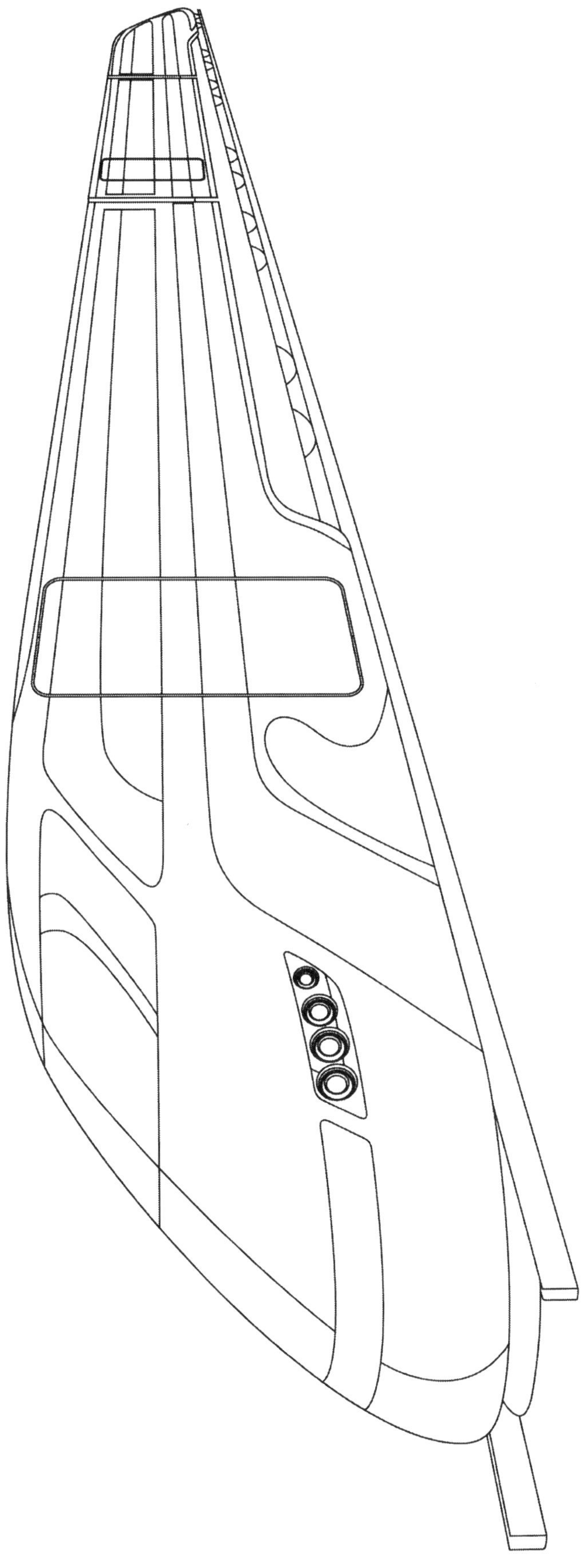

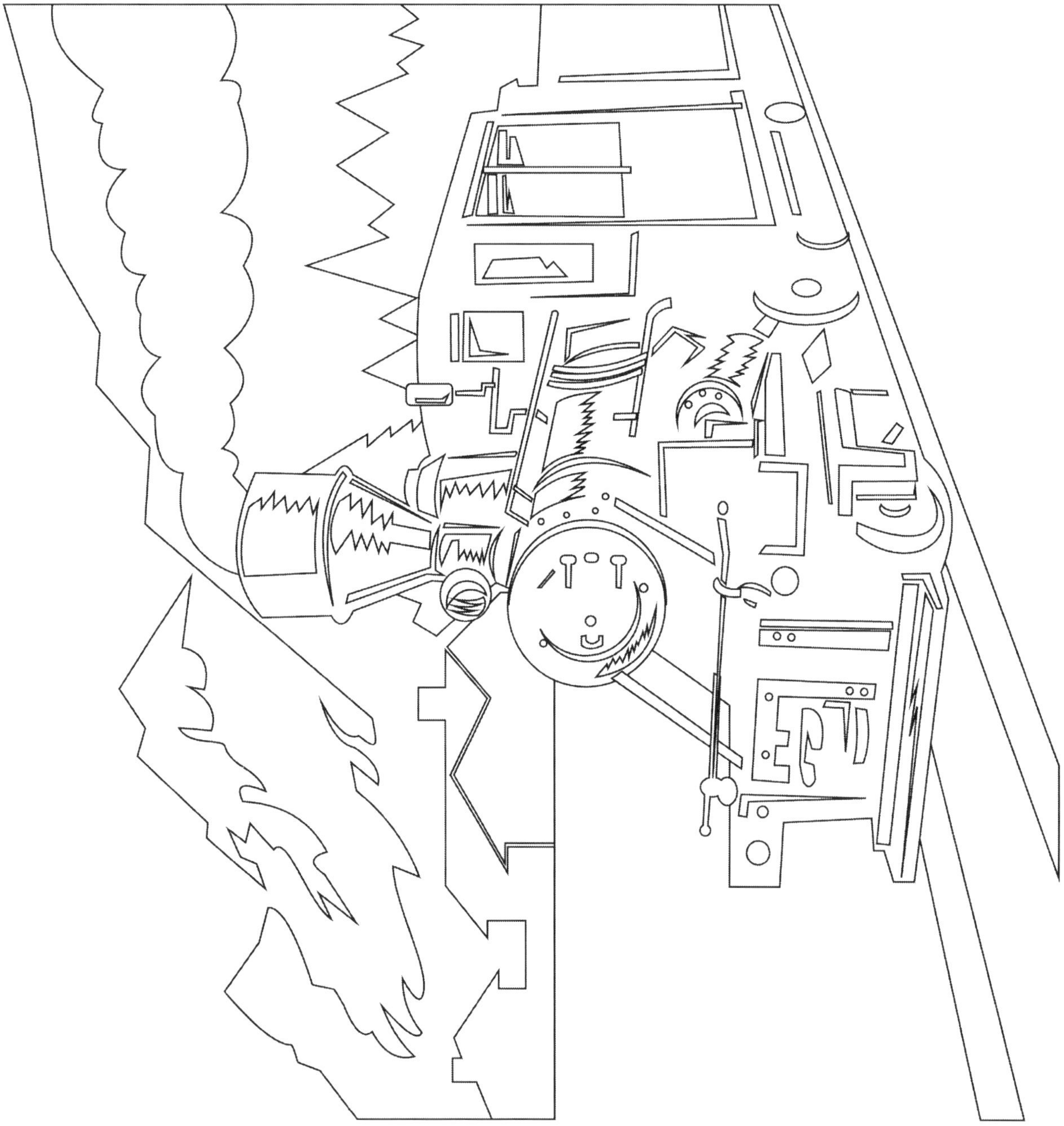

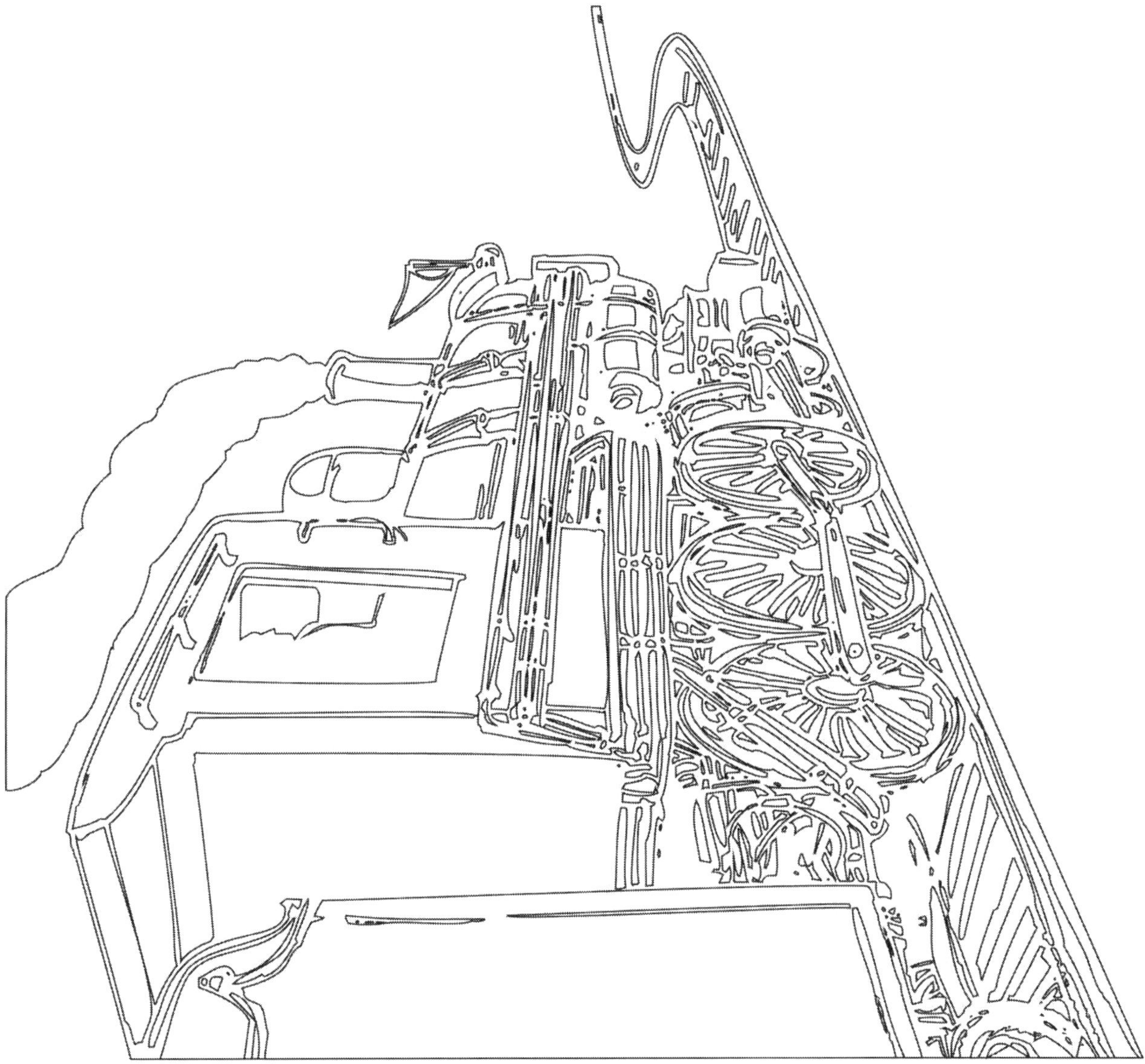

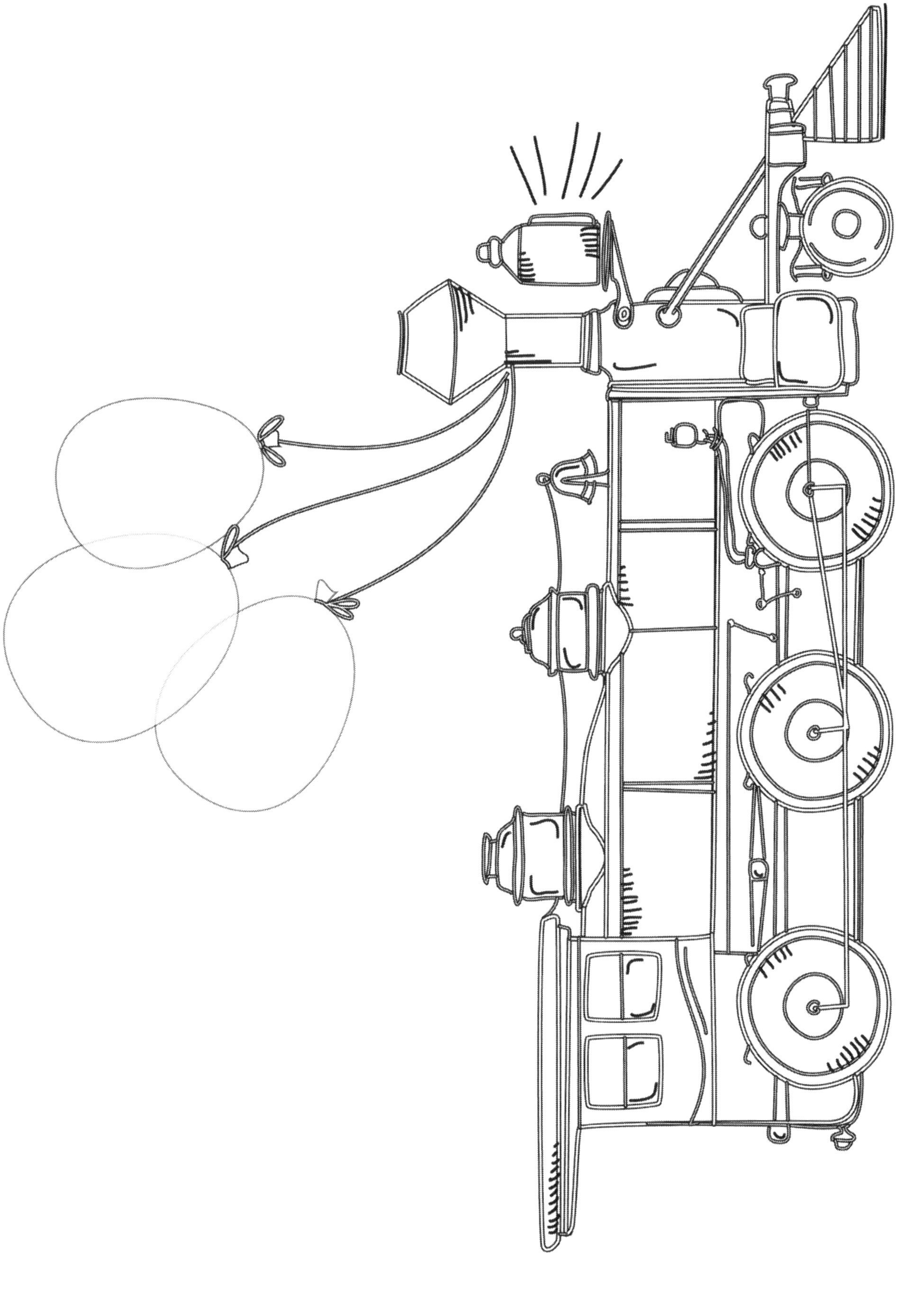

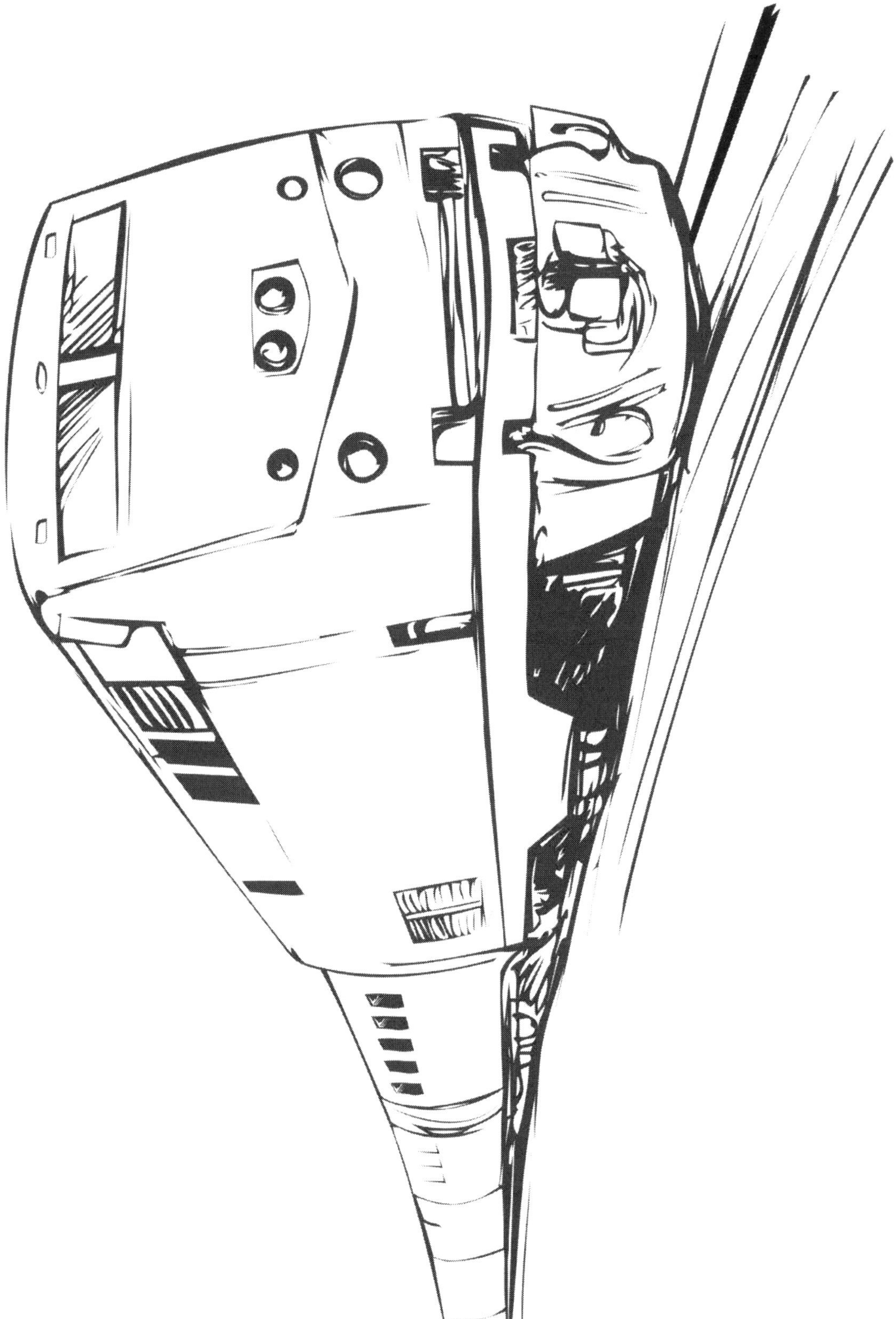

Made in the USA
San Bernardino, CA
29 November 2019

60592455R00027